EGO TO EARTHSCHOOL

Stephen Roxborough

rox. 2023

NeoPoiesisPress.com

herman james house 12:30

NeoPoiesis Press, LLC

2775 Harbor Ave SW, Suite D, Seattle, WA
Info@NeoPoiesisPress.com
NeoPoiesisPress.com

Stephen Roxborough
ISBN 978-0-9975021-6-9 (paperback: alk. paper)

   1. Poetry. I. Roxborough, Stephen. II. Ego to Earthschool.

Library of Congress Control Number: 2016961644

Design, art direction & typography:
Milo Duffin and Stephen Roxborough

Printed in the United States of America

for my mother

*thank you for teaching me
how to read*

you cant buy happiness but
youll die trying

pof.

contents

science

commerce

medicine

philosophy

intro to earthschool

there will be a test

much of the material is not in a book
or on a screen
                experience counts
for almost all of your grade

you are not your job
your job is to learn something
your job is to find out who you are
where you belong
how to get there
                mistakes are inevitable
            we encourage you to make a few

your will will be tested
in the end you will evaluate
& grade yourself
                most of the big questions
        have no specific practical answers
perhaps there are no right answers

did i mention earthschool isn't fair?
but it's like a great fair
so have some fun

your experience is all part
of the balance of the high-wire juggle
& razor's edge sword-swallow
the unhappy merry-go-round
& the holy-rollercoaster
the dream-flight the timeless clock
& first steps of the fire walk

your assessment will be re-evaluated
by an independent panel
& sent telepathically to your subconscious
as updates are needed or requested

please enjoy your stay

Humanities

folklore

according to folklore wild wolves raised
by the internet became even more wild

according to folklore when the music of mozart
was played to baby sequoias they matured
became mathematicians & later
transplanted to vienna

according to folklore if you sit too close to the TV
you'll be responsible for starting a war

according to folklore if you tell too many lies
you'll grow an old wives tail

according to folklore pluto is not a planet
but a funky caribbean island inhabited by sexy dancers
& fireball pitchers

according to folklore if a small boy has big feet
& large hands he'll grow a beard before his mother

according to folklore the raven talks so much
because she has an unlimited
cell phone plan

according to folklore early natives of las vegas
were born with one arm

according to folklore dreams answer
all the big questions
but many of the small questions
are more important

posterity is a bad audience

she doesn't listen
to you
        when you need it most
doesn't notice you until you're dead
& then plays hard to get
as if by then
there's anything to get

don't count on her to lift your dreams
above the grey loop of time
elevate a few shards
of your truth slash madness
to the elusive museum
of infinite mind

        it's all daDa! doo dah!!
doo daH!!!

some seem born with stars aligned
but even the brightest
                burn out
everything just moving through
this moment these words
this me this you

even posterity stumbles in & out of favor
sometimes crashes hard from grace

in the longest
        of the long run
she turns the most famous
of the famous

into inconsequence
& anonymous

interview (from a to b & back again)

a:
many people think you're putting them on
they say your work is a big joke
that you copy & reproduce & replicate
& that's all you can do
i mean do you feel misunderstood
don't you want to give them a different perspective
a different impression?

b:
i don't know i don't (pause) i don't think so
(longer pause) i don't really understand
the question

a:
that's okay i'll ask you some other questions
& you just say what pops into your head

b:
could you just give me the answers too

i think it would be better if you gave me
all the answers to the questions

a:
don't worry you'll loosen up
as we go along

b:
i'm serious i think you know the answers
better than i do

dere bill

i'm reading your book right now
your book TH BOOK now i'm reading
that book now
& finding it in my hands
holding it close to my body
in my bedroom bed
where i do most of my reading
& i'm finding your book a perfect reflection
of you & the times
you included all the epic themes
most of them
who are we? where do we come from? where
are we going? what do we do? is there
anything to do? why do we come here? what do we
do with life & death? until death
do us part
death appears to be less fun
than life but appearances
are deceiving   i'm thankful you leave it
open-ended another loophole in the narrative
my reflection in your reflection
i feel that connection
& i want you
to know you're getting through
you're calling me telepathically again
you're cutting through the mustard
the deep yellow the french's
the clutter of fluster
& cover
        into the airwaves you're slicing
& splicing through (has splicing become
a lost art yet?)
this never-ending wavelength
we decided to weave it into each other
the wave of rapture & suffer
of love & punctuation

i love how you put most of the punctuation
on six or ten pages
excellent idea
to show us punctuation stripped bare
unencumbered with grammatical purpose
of course wanting purpose
is part of the human condition
part of the reflection part of the whole
& why in part we are never whole
rarely whole
yet always holy
i'm reminded of an old joke
what did the buddha say to the hot dog vendor?
make me one with everything
that's what i feel like when i read
your books
one with everything
when you take me on train rides
let me smell the rain
taste the color orange & even paint
the sky with my eyes
as i'm reading your book
& finding everything
just like being in the supermarket
& the cashier sez *did you find everything?*
what a loaded question
i'm reading your new book
right now
wanted you to know
i love you & thank you
for writing this reflection for us all
to see ourselves & figure out a way to see
ourselves through
to thread ourselves through
the i
sometimes that's harder than it looks

like writing a great book
much easier to read a great book
than write one
so thanks for taking the time to invite us
on your train of thought
your poetry a perpetual beautiful
vehicle
& each trip with your words
a rich & raging
excursion

i took the near-famous poet

to the pub to quench his famous thirst
& i kept the pints flowing
while he graciously quietly steadily
methodically perused
my o so precious first manuscript

waited on tender hooks

as he stroked his white beard
to punctuate every turn of page
nod or phrase
               & finally
3 or 4 or 5 beers
later
with great certainty
proclaimed

your best poem
appears at the very beginning
he paused
       for another stroke
i believe you called it
he paused to quaff an ale
& order another
then turned to the precise page

i believe you called it
he repeated as i leaned closer

table of contents

fifty years

1,000 pages of poetry collected & edited
structured & translated & annotated
printed & bound between hard or soft covers
marketed reviewed & discounted
bought & sold as new & used
& sometimes read in beds before or after
sleep & dreams

& still the world is a collective mess
& still the children can't find their home on the globe
& still we drown ourselves in excrement & ignorance
& still we believe the news as if that's all there is
& still we don't meditate or mediate enough
& still we tow the line for the rich & powerful
& still we dreamwalk through life & death

with or without 1,000 pages of poetry
by a poet no longer chanting or ranting or raving
or hungry ghost starving for 1,000 pages of poetry
that made a small dent in the style of a genre
influenced popular music for more than 10 minutes
or shifted the psyche of a beat generation
of forgotten men & women beat by nature
& culture & time & looks good in your library
looks like you might know something
if it sits on your night table

but 1,000 pages of poetry doesn't wash
your underwear or dishes or automobile or brain
or feed the starving babies or share the wealth
of one thousand billionaires
or stop the chopping of forest
or the killing in the ocean
no

writing it reading it chanting it
or looking at it on your coffee table
won't change the world
but

1,000 pages of poetry is big enough
to break a window or start a fire or knock someone out
or use as a doorstop or press flowers
or stamps or beer labels or leaves of grass weapon

because 1,000 pages of poetry
stands on its own
in any shelf rack mantle stand or ledge
doesn't need to defend itself
will not go away without a fight
& probably last another century or two
who can say whether it was worth the effort
or time well spent
whether sound bytes or internet quotes
will carry it further or whether 1,000 pages
of poetry
could someday be
the perfect blessing or weapon

the famous author bought an autopen

it signs her books from remote locations
gives her the easy freedom of a mystic
to multi-task in more than one place

it writes inscriptions dedications
& the odd shopping list

it composes epic poems & curt emails
last weekend it wrote three chapters
of her next novel

it even composed an italian opera
while she sipped a fine bottle of wine

recently she installed a custom option
that changes her thoughts into screenplay
& sells it to hollywood for six figures

it cooks it cleans it dusts & vacuums
makes love in six languages
& dinner
in any cuisine you favor

it makes everything look so easy
one wonders how the poor & unknown
get anything done at all

everyone gets what they want

& no one is happy
how the party crashes
cause the cookie never crumbles in the middle
the lights come up too bright
& it's not very pretty

day breaks & there's not enough glue
in the world anymore

time to be alive or go back to sleep
not easy being a dreamer these days
even harder to wake up
from the dream

day breaks & there's not enough taboo
in the world anymore

everyone's trying to get home
but the heart of the home
has fallen apart
that chapter ripped out of the book
no more farmer's daughter
no more brick & mortar
no more old world order
my fingers are tired of walking

day breaks & there's not enough hullabaloo
in the world anymore

everyone gets what they want
& no one is happy
the lights come up bright
& it's not very pretty

the great flying fortified saucer pulsing plum jam spirit unification theory in a trembling eggshell poem bomb

we're all on the same path
at different stages of awareness
understanding hurt myth
mirth art faith mystery
                    truth
                    acceptance

contrary to needle-eye conditioning
the camel path
is super highway wide
abundance of energy
                    for everyone
                    climb on board!

this eternal procession moves
through us to realize
the depth of our ancient
brainwashing & squeegees
                    the film of thought
                    from third-eye windows

until we see the massive muddle
of concrete confusion
delusion that attracts & repels
& know everything is mostly
                    holy vibration
                    BOOM!

new work

a unique series of telepathic
poems
        promises to revolutionize
the publishing industry

hear they come now

the new old three-letter shell game

they got eyes in our screens
eyes on our beliefs & eyes on our Ps & Qs
they got eyes in our phones eyes in our tombs
& eyes right under your nose
they got eyes that recognize eyes that scandalize
eyes that disguise hypnotize & tell lies
the room is crawling with bugs
& even my fly-eyes are climbing the walls
they got eyes in the sky & eyes
on our fries & they even got eyes
in the back of our eyes

who the hell are they? who the hell are you?

their satellites pursue your every move
they hear you wheeze from the moon
your mail is monitored by lizards
with forked tongues & hair triggers
the drones in your home won't leave you alone
some bureaucrat with a persian cat
knows more about you than god
& they make you think you have friends
you never met as they invent another dimension
& pretend to hide inside the cloak
of prevention & protection

who the hell are they? who the hell are you?

bullets & bombs became obsolete
the fields of flanders now in cyberspace
& the race is on to steal your privacy
to make a dynasty on the backs of pirate society
because freedom is control & control depends on data
to peel away the layers of our taxpayer prayers
until they build a thousand firewalls to hell

here take a look your secrets are an open book
written by the hacker who knows everything
keeper of the code the worm the cyclops
the prism the mystic the stellar wind
the mole that repairs the endless
hole in your soulless matrix

who the hell are they? who the hell are you?

ego to earthschool

ego to earthschool
come in earthschool
do you read me? do you copy?
ego to earthschool
do you know how much i need to know?
will you be gentle? will you be kind?
will you be kind to the touch?
will you teach me too fast?
will it hurt when you teach me too much?

ego to earthschool
ego to earthschool
some say you learn all you need
to know in kindergarten
but i never heard a peep in the sandbox
about quantum physics
or what to do
when your heart grows bigger than your head
or why society pressures us
to trade substance & innocence
for the hive of daily grind

ego to earthschool
i'd make a better farmer
than a robot money grubber
ego to earthschool
once upon a time i got a secret tattoo
in a place you'll never find:
too grounded in nature
to climb the ladder
to nowhere

ego to earthschool
ego to earthschool
do you read me? do you copy?

ego to earthschool
every day another class another choice
another reason to question
another lesson to let go
ego to earthschool
ego to earthschool
i'm not too cool to play the fool
but most of the time
i'm just trying to find my notes
is there anything in them
anything more important to know
than how to lose my ego in earthschool
ego to earthschool
ego to earthschool
come in earthschool
i'm dull & soft & lost & old
i'm baked & fried & tired & cold
can i spend some time on easy street
or is that just a roll of the dice?
how much life will that cost
is it ever worth the price?

ego to earthschool
ego to earthschool
do you read me? do you copy?
a thousand angels with a million
lessons & reasons
swirl around us
waiting to ride inside us
may the great teachers always guide us
away from the fray
of the flags of confusion

ego to earthschool
ego to earthschool
do you read me? do you copy?

i used to study the field of philosophy
seemed to improve my inner psychology
until i shot it down with angry ideology
then my isms & ologies all
washed away
one perfect summer day
by the poetry of love

ego to earthschool
ego to earthschool
do you read me? do you copy?
o holy earthschool
save me from myself
just when i think i know what's going on
something else much worse goes down
my answers breed more questions
& all those needy children
want more & more attention

ego to earthschool
ego to earthschool
come in earthschool
come in earthschool
do you read me?
do you copy?

how to be cool without a tattoo

be yourself be natural
be comfortable with the skin
you're in
      your tribe is the universe
& cool don't grow on skin
cool always comes
from within

love yourself be natural
you're better than good enough
but if you must
         in vogue we trust
buy yourself a funky hat
walk with a rhythm stick
strut some swag
be cool as a cat
read a cosmic book
respect your epidermis
expand the corners of your mind
travel beyond the surface
make a brand new
rhyme

be natural be yourself
be comfortable with the skin you're in
your tribe is the universe
& cool don't grow on skin
go as you please & come as you are
there's really nothing to win
love yourself be natural
cool always comes
from within

persistent side effects will occur

you will pay & then you will pay some more
& after that you will endure fees &
taxes & fines & dues

all the while you will accrue hidden costs
for example but not limited to
illness accident & aging
however if you live life to the fullest
you will make mistakes
& there will be karma & dogma to pay

always bills bills bills from banks & stores
& credit card jail & impulsive late night
on-line sales & food & booze
& drugs & pub hell & hi-fi & wi-fi &
private eye & humble pie

you will also experience random acts of god
& war & environmental disaster &
cancer & crazy people with guns & bombs
& political power
which will lead to confusion & conspiracy
& rising prices & falling dollar &
lost wages & reduced buying power

there will be deductions & seductions
addictions & restrictions
sorrow & sorry & worry & woe
laws & rules & punishments you don't know
until it's too late

there will be toys & gadgets & widgets
& shiny sparkly things that always break
or become lost or stolen

if you get lucky you could fall in love
& marry & have children & live in bliss

for a few years before divorce
& lawyers take their pound of flesh
as they rip you apart
but in the end
you always pay more with your heart

in a flash your investments crash
for no reason except they always do
unless you can afford to buy great art
then you've won the game
when you understand
what's priceless from the start

money is timing & timing is everything
& you will pay dearly if you must
have everything
but you can't buy timing

as your children grow you will pay more
& more & they will have accidents &
make mistakes & you will pay
& feel more & more for them
because you love them more than yourself
& that says something important
about being an everyday parent

over & over & over the same refrain
over & over & over the same chest pain
over & over & over the same dog chain
over & over & over the same tail-chasing reign
over & over & over the same blinding migraine
over & over & over the same material plane
that drones on & on & on
you will pay
& then
you will pay some more

forgotten explorer

he's the han solo don quixote of the sea
headed into uncharted waters
                with oceans to cross
& rum to ration
pirates to curse & scurvy to fight
exotic lands to plunder
& self-mutiny to navigate

        yet he never lifts his anchor
        never leaves the bay

logically methodically steers
his steady ship in circles
one direction at a time
always the same scenery
& the same destination
            even unfavorable winds
will take him there

        sometimes he starts the motor
        to hear her perfect gurgle

reminds him of bathtub play
lips half-underwater
a long time ago

breaking clichés

sometimes you gotta break a few commandments
to make an omelette

when life
            hands you lemons
                        make a margarita

i could give you a fish & feed you for a day
but if i taught you how to fish
you might
            die of mercury poisoning

which came first: the chicken or the chicken
mcnugget?

the grass is always greener
unless you're looking through
a black & white filter

when you wish upon a bone you gotta wonder
if that animal still has a sense of humor
about human superstition

everything is relative except for your relatives

you can lead a writer to the bar
but you can't make him pick up the tab

you don't know what you got till it's gone
& then after a few days you forget about it
because something else is missing

sometimes you gotta break a few clichés
to create a new thought pattern

snippets (the lost art of lost conversation)

anything overheard in a dream
on the street watching TV or clouds
the rules there are no rules
anyone with two glass eyes can see
he's right & i'm wrong
sambuco is my rapper name
who do you hate more: the americans or
the americans?
the locksmith unlocked her chastity belt
she's still got her tattoos
nothing is ever all good or all bad
i see what you're saying but i don't want to smell it
in a perfect world all the women
are beautiful rich & blind
the possibilities are always endless
bob dylan's unintelligible words are overrated
looking under a rock & finding nothing
is still progress
she's got tons of cleavage
it's not worth anything until you sell it
just because you want to do it
doesn't make it a poem
i used to be in a band called whatever
prevention is nine tenths of the law
a coffee cup full of tears
the ocean full of plastic the fish full of plastic
& soon you will be too
meanwhile in the south of france
let me check my spam
i need to start following my own advice
how many posts does it take
to make a post-modern?
the answers to that are i don't know
i don't know & i don't want
to know

near here a famous person once lived

the facade of the building
an interpretive reconstruction
nothing authentic left

the name of the street changed
the addresses defunct
the sidewalk an approximation
of where anyone ever stood
          even the memory of fame lost

some say he was a great writer
yet none of his important books
can be found
          others say she was a scientist
who discovered something so far ahead
of her time
the breakthrough lost
in the shuffle
              of the patent office

we can only imagine how extraordinary
this person might have been

this one-time residence
a home to ordinary people
trying to make

ends meet

www

we weave a new-fangled web
& loom to repeat
history

grandfather was a canoe carver

hollowed & shaped tree spirits
made large trunks of dense red wood
laugh & dance over turbulent ocean

one day he told me the secret
of his art came from watching the river
listening to the harmony of water
then waiting
for the perfect leaf
to fall into the eternal flow
where the life force
of all creatures dwells

this unique leaf showed him the shape
of a better vessel
to carry warriors to battle
return plundered treasures home
lift the courage & pride of the tribe
inspire new songs & fantastic dance
exalt victory & respect defeat
make heroes of regular men
& men of young boys

precisely then i realized
all the magnificence of my male ancestors
flows from the silent beauty
of a fallen leaf
& it was my grandfather's job
to know & follow
this tradition

the surrealist hitman

fear motivates him to keep working
keep breathing keep over-eating keep severing
relationships
keep to himself

swallow hard gasp choke cough wheeze

he's a near-perfect paranoid he believes
& then gets paranoid about the pitfalls
of being almost perfect
                although he has no evidence
        he knows this poem
is about him

his greatest fear is insects
he sees ants with microscopic vision
imagines their snapping jaws
waiting to devour him

he declines all invitations to picnic
or drive in the country
fabricates elaborate excuses
                        to avoid nature

lives downtown surrounded by concrete banks
& pest exterminators

he figures humans will eventually
suffocate themselves
& large winged insects will take over

for now he feels safe
in the city

alone

uncommon common courtesies

please & thank you & i'm sorry
& you're welcome & i apologize
& pardon me & after you & excuse me
& bless you & hello how are you
& yes right away & yes sir & yes ma'am
& no thank you & yes please & thank you
very much & thank you so much
& pretty please & pretty please
with a cherry on top & i don't know
but i'll find out & glad to be of service
& good to see you again & nice
to meet you & make yourself comfortable
& make yourself at home & can i get you
anything & is everything all right
& let me fix that for you & don't worry
about a thing & life is full of surprises
& yes of course we'll take care of that
straight away & no worries & consider it
done & as you wish & thank you for
the pleasure of serving you & we hope
to see you again & see you soon
& see you real soon &
please come back &
until we meet again & thank you
for everything & fare thee well
& godspeed & goodbye

his poetry has been translated into

86 languages
most of them oral
four are gastrointestinal
one of them in serious condition
& may never recover from
the experience

still it's a fine thing
to be translated into many languages
although there's no way
of knowing
if they got the poem right

much can be lost in translation

i wonder if new stanzas
have ever been discovered
in a new translation

or if in some languages
a poem finds a life of its own
gets a mild case of plagiarism
& runs away
with another poet

finis

the revolution ended when we bought all the toys
& ran out of political disgust
the revolution ended at the first shake
of the earthquake
                    after the fall of the dust
        & the rust of scruples crushed
the revolution ended when we got old & fat & lazy
when they gave us just enough power
& invited us to dinner
in a newer bigger imitation ivory tower

the revolution ended when we ran out of butter
bullets & future
then we all got arrested
our foundations became twisted
& we realized jail was worse than work
the revolution ended when the system
became the solution
                    & the solution became the system
& the system became the institution
the institution of delusion

the revolution ended when they pulled the plug
on the internet
& everything naturally updated
in perfect disconnect
we screamed for our screens
but there was nothing left
to protect
        the revolution ended when they gave us
free beer
told us to drink up
be humble be thankful
someday your leader might become prime minister
then thoughts became nursery crimes

the revolution ended when we forgot
how to grow our own
& became dedicated to the shopping spree
then we ran out of water & our parents saw us
on TV
          the revolution ended when the military
destroyed our global image & the tasers came to town
we stopped having babies
& started watching touchdowns

the revolution ended when it got too hot to fight
nothing became what we pretended
& no one remembered how to halluncinate
fantasize visualize or imagine
anymore
          religion promised us heaven
          & heaven was a bottle of spirits
the revolution ended when violence became revolting
& we got dizzy spinning our wheels
in the quicksand

the revolution ended when they gave us
government jobs
we all made too much money
& our children took up arms against us

the revolution ended when fighting
wasn't worth the fight

the revolution ended when we became our parents
all the frogs died
the cows came home to roost
the old dogs coudn't stop farting
& the big clock stopped

the revolution ended when we lost our vision
& forgot we could still read & write &
dream

Science

everything once poured

into one giant gumbo
permanently fermenting & blending
& stirred for ages of eons
until wonder bubbled to surface
grew legs
& walked out of the cauldron

the creation of creation
clearly a very messy business
unpredictable & chaotic
order never wins
because order is boring repetitive
dull droning tedious
give me chaos!
the spice of inspired life

crank up the almighty heat

let's see who needs another
fast mustache glass of milk

we're all just ghost peppers
happily swimming in the ooze
of soupy dimension
molecules
        dissolving
                into spirit

then released into ecstatic steam
& heavenly sky

drink up & stay thirsty my friends
the secret essence of a better recipe
might take another
4 billion years

darwin's finches

all muted colored
from the same island group
drab black or brown
        beaks define them
size strength shape
what they eat
how they get their food
often overlapping into the range
of another species

tree finches ground finches
specific island finches
small medium large finches
cactus woodpecker mangrove
vegetarian warbler
& hybrid finches

        odd they call them finches
when they're not true finches
their ancestry split
as if mighty moses parted
        the gene pool
not even clear which family
they belong to

but they can join my family
i'll adapt & adopt them anyday
deep down we're all related
to function
       & dysfunction

ode to plumbers

every civilization collapses
in ruin without
          someone to organize pipes
keep tap & toilet water separate
& flowing

praise to the fitters & fixers of flow
the diverters of fertilizer & stench
to the sweet smell of fresh
& clean
to the unseen unwanted unwelcome fruit
of their labors

glory to the tools & trade of sacred sanitation
their blessed wrenches
holy hack saws & trusty pliers

glory to their divine files & reliable augers
their flaming torches
humble hammers & loyal plungers

reverence to their faithful cracks
& tolerant noses

let us ring & resonate sacred praise
to every righteous plumber!

true captains of good health
& superior culture

poetry matters

                because it doesn't matter
the physics of anti-matter

poetry cannot be squandered like currency
you cannot abuse the muse
to make money
              especially free verse

who can prove anything with words & rhyme
you cannot price tag syntax or spread
enjambment on your toast

poetry is found in the wide belts of gaseous giants
poetry opens portals in the cracks of normal
who can sustain anything as a prisoner
of closed mind & rigid symbol

poetry matters because it doesn't matter

because nature abhors a vacuum
because you can't have one
without the other

uncertainty principle

thank god it's friday again
even though it feels like tuesday

if i convince myself long enough
time will return to thursday

i know it's not saturday
space never points to saturday

saturday doesn't have to try too hard.
saturday just is

wednesday   drifts by
inside of monday or sunday

hard to tell from this angle
why the calendar is so confused

grids gone haywire & twisted
prime numbers melt into composite

even the man on the street perplexed
sand slips through his plans

in a forgotten frame somewhere
green apples rain on bowler hats

if i retrace my steps fast enough
everything might slow down

the shortest distance between two lines

is a point
not polite to point
my mother liked to point out
what's your point? said my father
point me in any direction
good point bad point fair point
fine point dull point
finger pointing
pointless
point

most points wins
west point is in the east
letting go is the point of least resistance
the shortest point between two lines
is your imagination
on point off point
appointed by her majesty
the queen

if life is pointless
why is this pain so sharp?
all points bulletin: nothing points
to everything
point of fact point of fiction
not sure i get your point
learn to the point of remembering
then learn to the point
of forgetting
when all points fail
there's always the point
of no return

if i could

the world is now weary again
her shoulders slumped her underground
energy drained
her mettle spent her wounds wound
too tight for too long

if i could i'd invite her inside for a glass of wine
& a fireside massage
slow down her centrifugal force
read her poetry from a long lost century
tilt her axis to release the pressure
unwind her poles unravel her knots
align her plates & listen
to the musical moans of letting go

i'd bribe the moon to coax her tides
to pull us closer
take us both to a timeless place
where matter fuses & space expands
where burdens become light
& numbers
can't be counted

where gravity has no currency
the way home is through the heart
& busyness goes on a long
long easy aimless
vacation

hour of the fallow plow

this hour of the fallow plow
moves through
our sleep

everything tosses & turns
every cell in hum & vibration
in & without holy tune
every grain yearning
for song

old man landscape snores
& shakes worry
from roots

we spin as if we know
where we're going
as if we know anything at all
as if there is even anything
to know

random waves pierce bubbles
nothing really ever
the same

nothing repeats itself
nothing repeats itself exactly
nothing ever exact
this hour of the fallow plow
lopes & lingers

this hour of the fallow plow
moves through
our dreams

44

scientists made a 3-D model of

the galaxy cluster in our corner
of the universe he said

what does it look like she said
what shape does it have?

it has a lot of curves he said
lots of crazy-making wavy curves

men see everything in curves she said

perhaps god can't make a straight line he said

perhaps there's no such thing as
                    a straight line she said

ahhhhhhh the illusion of linear he said
the solutions of curves she said

the best models he said have curves
the best curves she said
are universal

kinesis

the spheres in their orbits

      the galaxies in their swirls

the comets in their ellipses

      the workers in their routines

the clocks in their sprockets

      the hands in their sweeping

even the random minds
                    of lovers
   make a pattern

on the cosmic roundabout

         kisses & invoices
   pile up

tailchasing continues

the space between his ears

became greater than anyone
could know

he opened ordinary doors
to magic portals
        passed through dirty windows
into perfect wormholes

folded time & laundry on itself

painted his mind in sunrise sky
mixed colors so deep
the whole ocean
fit into a single brushstroke

invented a telescope so powerful
he could see the back
of his head

                        stopped wars
with a song too beautiful
to destroy
        embraced the lonely
in a cosmic hug
& expanded the universe
with a sneeze

even his bad dreams worked
for the greater good

on & on & on & on the space
between his ears never stopped
moving
        down the lost
superhighway

have you ever seen a molecule?

i mean up close & personal
in color with sharp focus

every image i see is fuzzy & makes me wonder
if it's a coffee stain on a napkin
or if i'm stuck in some hazy cartoon world

do molecules have edges or are they made of curves?
do they come in a variety of colors? are they
subject to mood swings?
is their bonding full of pleasure?
are their break-ups painless?

can molecules communicate? have a sixth sense?
do they make sound? or vibrate at a frequency
beyond earthly ears?

are they ever happy?

do molecules know their neighbors? do they dream
of fission or fusion? are they part of the problem
or part of the solution?

do molecules get atom-envy?

do parts of you wear out? do your electrons
ever hurt? do you never stop for a nap
or take a tiny vacation?

are molecules born to die?

or is matter just another part of our imagination?
can a molecule be tamed?
i don't think so

but thinking is often the worst way
to approach discovery

waiting

a gift
that slows
    the clock

      beautiful opportunity
to dance

between the tick
    inside the tock

        one moment

    at a time

what doesn't kill me makes me

wonder if death is a toothless illusion
designed to make us
suffer
the same oozing wound
over & over
until we learn
to slow down the unmerry-go-round
& stop giving our mistakes
too much power

what doesn't kill me makes me
wonder why
          we focus on so many things
outside ourselves
when everything we need
is readymade
& built-in

what doesn't kill me makes me
stronger but you don't need much muscle
to know
you haven't reached
your limit yet

you'll never fathom the top
or the bottom
                    so just keep going
          one step at a time
& you'll do fine

especially when you realize
there never was
a finish line

you are what you wear

after hundreds of millions of dollars of decades of research
fashion scientists finally understand the psychology
of colors

for instance red symbolizes dominance passion
sensuality
& dark juvenile masochistic clown violence

peach & pink express the inner rejection of homophobic
impotence whereas brighter whites reflect
a clanlike obsessive compulsion
toward racism

black represents death power religion
& diet soft drinks

blue is the true color of trust & dysfunction
yellow conveys anxiety yet heightens the secret pleasures
of vertigo

green epitomizes irresponsibility & jealousy
orange makes you more demanding
brown is a reliable color for comfortable shoes
& sloppy eaters
purple is the color of inbred royalty
heartburn & ruthless arrogance

don gray cloth & you're sophisticated
yet thankfully mediocre

wear desert camouflage in a temperate rain forest
& it's obvious you have progressive gender confusion
with compounded interest in roulette

polka dots exude a willingness to get drunk

argyle socks offer bad stock market tips on purpose
whereas stripes deceive even themselves

old perspective

sometimes when he made a list
of things to do
he set the bar too low
usually
included
drink a few beers
&
don't answer the phone

sometimes he avoided mirrors
for weeks at a time
just to see if he'd notice
how ungracefully
he was aging

sometimes he judged himself against
shakespeare
&
mozart
then suddenly realized that was unfair
because they didn't have multiple screens
to distract & get lost in

sometimes he'd go outside at night
look up at the stars
&
think
how come i'm so big
& they're so small

sometime near the end of oil

before the numbers got real & drastic
we gave a modest thumbs up
to the expoitable convenience
of disposable plastic

didn't seem like much at the time
a razor here a water bottle there
premeditated garbage
nothing but a quiet incidental
environmental crime

the prognosis for mass hypnosis
o please don't tell us
what we don't want to know
        instead let's bury our heads
in the beach
until we can't escape
part of the new landscape
that won't go away

it's big & small it's short & tall
& lives longer than we do
it brushes our teeth & hair
it cradles mother's milk
& gathers cans of father's beer
it flies & drives & floats
it's colorful & clear
on shorelines oceans & landfills
even in our virgin air
it walks like jesus on our holy water
it's everywhere! it's everywhere!

three cheers for the throw away
that's here to stay
so fantastic it's metastatic
        hip hip hurray hip hip hurray
hip hip hurray for plastic!

every time the future sweeps the country

we look cleaner but all feel
a little dirtier

tomorrow is a program designed for control
the perfect rinse cycle to repel
& rebel
   warm & bubbly speeches
   from the latest fearless leader

lead us not into temptation
but into viral fear & social media
into armies of bugs & drones
commanded by henchmen
from crafty acronyms
run on ones
   & zeroes

new improved superior heartlessness
now sweeping the heartland
scrubbing the landscape
brainwashing
our human
laundry

until shampooing thoughtcrime
the new clean

& a shower is not a shower

the zen of waiting

each fall he waited
for the trees in his yard to empty
their leaves from the aching bones
of reaching branches
watch them float drift & spin
to ground
& wait some more

wait for autumn rains to fall
then wait for the sun to come out
dry the soggy fronds & wait
for the neighbor's leaves to blow
over into his yard & wait
for bigger winds to whoosh
them into the street

then wait for unknown cars
to grind twigs & veiny skins
into mulch & dirt & dust
& wait at last
for the city street-sweeper
rolling a big hardbristle brush
scatter scoop & suck 'em up
for safe keeping

while he & his trusty rake
prop themselves on the front porch
kick back
with the best view of neighbors
chasing suburban dreams
with leaf blower plastic bag
consciousness

& watch the wheels go
round & round

another sad case

hands up!
your development is
under arrest

no rest for edgar

when the city of baltimore
decided edgar allen poe's final resting place
was too humble for a trailblazing
visionary globally acclaimed author
they raised enough hard cash
for a large stone marker
& a rich man's plot

the perfect irony for an artist
who struggled
for modest financial acceptance
& died
in the gutter
of unknown causes

yet when the whistling grave digger
unearthed & moved
poe's coffin
a distinct disquieting rattle
at the head of the box
gave him a start
an eerie remark from a writer
who used sound to punctuate surprise
& elevate horror

today doctors know a brain anyeurism
causes greymatter to harden
into a small ball inside
the skull

one last laugh from the master
of macabre

commerce

trade

we trade life energy
for the abstract of currency
giving our labor the power to buy whims
& fashion callous skins
that rile nature
   in return we pay triple
   to live so unnatural
  to realize we've all been used
to maintain the ruse of getting & spending
& working neverending
   we're only tiny teeth
  on the material cog
  of the wheel for the machine
that drives the dream
to layer the matrix of perpetual
fractal
   a billion carrots cannot buy your way
   off this cosmos of cycle
& recycle
around & around we tailspin
this brainwashing phase
of original sins
   log that forest those hours
   that logarithm log on
log in
hectic chaotic
dizzy crazed busy bees
for the money
our honey almighty
   what goes around comes a round
   spiral up & corkscrew down
tragically happy
with the magic of gravity
tragically happy
with the fantasy of sanity
repeat repeat rinse
repeat

trust

never trust anyone over 30
never trust anyone under 50
never trust a slogan
never trust a promise from a politician
never trust those who trust the network news
never trust a bluffing blind man
never trust in god we trust
never trust a military recruiter
never trust an untroubled troubleshooter
never trust a bald headed barber
never trust the value of a dollar

never trust anyone who says
                    you can trust me
never trust a jungle animal
never trust an urban cannibal
never trust a stripper with your financial affairs
never trust a peg-leg pirate
never trust perfect hair
never trust a knuckleball
never trust musical chairs
never trust dinner at a diner called mom's
never trust a syndicate of cons

never trust anyone who claims
                    i have all the answers
never trust a fortune cookie
never trust a room without windows
never trust a house without books
never trust a bar full of hippos
never trust a tibetan roadblock
never trust a perfect robot
never trust the man in the moon
never trust a pie chart
never trust the end of the rainbow
never trust a silent fart

never trust a teenage philosopher
never trust one-size-fits-all
never trust a preacher with his own TV show
never trust a man without a vice
never trust a bordeaux from a faux chateau
never trust a hurricane with a guy's name
never trust a businessman who says
            it's not about the money
never trust opinion based on opinion
never trust a tearless onion

never trust an asterisk without a footnote
never trust a skinny chef
never trust a sleeping crocodile
never trust a flooded road
never trust a dead man in denial
never trust a sober wino
never trust the clock at work
never trust a confident weatherman
never trust a generalization
never trust a deal too good to be true
never trust anyone who says
            let me be honest with you

never trust a dentist who begins
            this won't hurt a bit
never trust perfection
never trust 20 questions
never trust the corner of your eye
never trust your head in bed
never trust the light at night
never ever trust happily ever-after
never trust forever
never trust never
never trust never

edgy benediction

let us pray let us pray
let us prey on the weak-minded
disciples of advertising & political
propaganda
give us this day our daily gluten-free
sour dough ancient grain
unleavened dread
the non-stop blues of news
the holy horror & terror
in the name of depraved religion
or any other unnatural system
forgive our debts
our insecticides & genocides
our GMOs & designer clothes
our nuclear waste & expanding waistlines
forgive our stupid smart bombs & F-bombs
& drones in heaven droning on & on
forgive our invasions
& occupations
even though we cannot forgive those
who trespass against us
but lead us not into temptation
unless there's serious money to be made
& deliver us better pizza
in less than 30 minutes
by condom cum thy will done
on earth as it is at 7-eleven
for strong cheap wine
is the kingdom's power & glory
forever & ever
amen
& women
if it weren't for the men & women
we wouldn't need
the wine

cosmic slingshot

canada throws her panties
into the sky
           they twist tumble
   & turn
into a crazy raven
that swoops down & steals the moon
from my eye

tonight the heavens crowd
with blazing stars

billions of godlike furnaces raging
at the dark feathers
      & magic sapphire sheen

our only home looks small
from here

      our miniature blue-eyed
blind cyclops marble
spinning wild

& naked
          flying headless
     into space

money worry blues

the landlord changed
the locks on my door
the women i love
don't know me anymore

my 52 credit cards
are charged to the max
i'm uptight because
it costs too much to relax

my insurance man sez
you're worth more dead than alive
the bank wants my blood
but they done bled me dry

the high cost of air
keeps me out of breath
worry for money
a new kind of death

worry for money
a new kind of death

what eden became

the pain the hurt the blame
the suffering the mind the dream
the pain
      the blame the illusion the disillusion
the confusion the pain the hurt
the blame the suffering
              the mind
the dream the time the clock
the years
      the dream
the number the mind the wonder
the answer the world
the column the account the dream
the wave the rush the blood
the ocean
      the drop the fall
the impact
the pain the hurt the grace
              the blame
the suffering the mind
the dream
      the dream

soon

there will be no great wars
or great war heroes
there will only be perpetual conflicts
of disinterest & petty officers
who take orders
from billionaires who never
go to war
never suffer a skirmish
outside their lily-white boardrooms

& soon is here too soon

they drop bags of money not bombs
yet there goes the neighborhood
there goes landscape
all the same

& soon is here too soon

the prophet we seek is not in coin
the power not in winning

soon all the answers will come
to us like fortune cookies
falling from the sky
raining bytes
of shallow restaurant
wisdom

& soon is here too soon

the greatest threat

to our western way of life
is our western way of life

the first glass of wine

made me wince & swallow hard
figured i was taken
but i paid seven dollars
for this bogus-bordeaux
from the highlands
of new jersey
so i had to have a second glass
& now i'm positively sure
it's my last nip
but confidentially
the night is young
& i'm aging gracefully
so i talk myself into forcing
a third glass down
& ever so slowly the tide turns
the bouquet opens up
to a complex nose of surgical spirit
the imagination of my tastebuds
now full of rancid blackberry
& stale coffee
notes of fresh mowed grass
old shoe leather
soft pencil lead from the 19th century
& before i know it
i'm drinking it straight from the bottle
hell it already comes in a glass
damn i swear to myself
the juice is all gone
& suddenly i'm convinced
that's the best seven dollars
i ever spent in my life

when is more more

when is less more when is more less
is enough ever enough?

      the artist the businessman
the athlete the mother the father the guru
the moon the farmer the sun the hunter
the actor the student the star
the stardust
the gambler the musician the muse
the magician the mathematician
the chef the soldier the salesman the judge
the teacher the singer the siren
the vortex the system the politician
the portal the poet the pilot the pirate
the president
the house painter the jokester
the pontif the thief
the roaster the trickster the doctor
the overtime undertaker
& priest

      all programmed to want more
& more as if enough
is never enough
as if more
is the god we trust

business for the brainless

the most famous chicken
in the world
a wyandotte rooster named mike
lived for 18 months
after his head was cut off

he balanced on a perch
walked clumsily
even attempted to preen & crow
unaware that neither activity
could be accomplished
without a pate

at the height of mike's popularity
he earned in admission costs
the equivalent
of $50,000 a month
from 25 cents a head

how shallow our brainless skulls
brimming with consequence
& mindless crave
how imperfect our relationship
with ourselves

idolatry

six stories high
made of plastic foam
& fiberglass

the king of kings statue
also known as
the touchdown jesus

built for 250,000 dollars
as a beacon of hope
& salvation

with long referee arms
reaching to the heavens
struck last night

by the hand of god
flamed & charred
into holy ghost

the morning after the death of apology

we mourned all the sorrys
that never could be
drank ourselves into eternity
& realized how each generation
loses the same compass
over & over again

this funeral a wake & a dream

seems the race to the bottom
never ends
we believe too much in ourselves
& little of anything else
bottoms up & anchors away

this funeral a wake & a dream

they say the death of regret
is coming next week
& then there's no turning back
eventually we'll kill it all
only winter can break
this fall

this funeral a wake & a dream

& the bottom is still
& the bottom is still
dead quiet dream drunk
a long long long way down

the bottom is still
a very long way down

original instructions

the light of stars
powers the plan of planets
revolving & evolving the great place
of spirit
where the orbits of comets
meet the reflection of moons
as everything corkscrews
through space
from the inside out
spinning & ringing & tripping & turning
distinctively vibrating gyrating
& migrating
instinctively knowing & sowing
the seeds of flora
& fauna

        for food & cloth & home
for water & river & ocean
for sky & cloud & lungs
for seasons hot & cold
for weather wet & dry
for east & west & north & south
for beauty & glory & harmony
everything alive with heartbeat & breath
everything great & related
connected & flowing together
into the bigger & mirrored
picture

        everything following original plan
every mountain & valley & grain of sand
everything except the tightfisted
twisted man
who takes more than he needs
& makes more than he gives
who removes himself from greens & blues

& escapes into the illusion
of user & computer
who thinks he protects himself
from disaster with ones & zeroes
& fence & border & wall
with prison & mission & villain
& millions of imitation isms
with guns & bombs & bullet-proof vest
with crowd & cloud & climate control
& droning roaming glowing eyes
in the sky

    when all we really need is
to believe in the simplicity & synchronicity
of our original instructions:
be kind & peaceful
be generous & thankful
let us see & hear without judgement or fear
let us listen with both ears to the ground
& our hearts in our heads

    let us practice letting go
of the strings & all material things
that weave the want & taunt
into our webs
        let nature be our mother
        our leader & our rudder

    let nature be our mother
    our healer & our wonder

let nature be our mother
our teacher & our power

business is business

shine your shoes trim split ends
dress for market trends & dividends
shake hands with your 5-year plans
sell yourself to prophets with deep pockets
from japan to buckingham & new amsterdam
but don't get blinded by the bling
of a sun king from beijing
who can make a bottom line sing?
who can make a bottom line sing?

balance the ledgers of imbalance
offset receivables & payables
with unbelievables & inconceivables
stoke the furnace of greed for the nation
expand the loopholes of tax evasion
divide to multiply & conquer
it don't mean a thing if it ain't got that
capital sting
who can make a bottom line sing?
who can make a bottom line sing?

numb the world with numbers
join private clubs with shady members
learn to lie like a toupee under oath
predict the future of exponential growth
take a trillion times more than you give
& learn to smell blood in the boardroom
it's only a primal survival
predatory thing
who can make a bottom line sing?
who can make a bottom line sing?

get obsessed with the process of success
tally your net worth to the penny
more & more begets never enough
until excess is too obvious to suppress

you can't buy happiness but you'll die trying
it's a fat cat bureaucrat top hat diplomat
new tycoon thing
      who can make a bottom line sing?
      who can make a bottom line sing?

MEDICINE

they say readers make better lovers

their relationships are deeper
& last longer
readers are more patient
better listeners more verbal stronger conversationalists
their curiosity & imaginations more expansive
their fantasies become more real
& suddenly
with minimal effort
readers become more intelligent
more compassionate
much sexier
especially to other readers
          they say readers are less vain
& self-centered
less likely to go to jail
be crucified or get beheaded
they say readers age more gracefully
feel less hurried
or worried
live more in the moment & orgasm
two point two times a week
          they say readers eat at better restaurants
watch better movies & travel
to more stimulating destinations
they say readers have better
vocabularies
express themselves with less inhibition
& less frustration with the world
even though they know more about it
or perhaps because
they know more about it
          they say when you pick up a book
a real book made of paper ink stitching or glue
& sit in a comfortable chair
or recline on the grass
          or the soft warm sand

                    of a faraway beach
or even under the covers
of a lover's bed
            your blood pressure stabilizes
an air of flawless confidence
calmness & pleasure
envelope you wash over you
become you

bodysurfing with gandhi

the wave machine pool
with the faux burmese
jungle motif
in the middle
of the mohave desert
almost hollywood surreal
until i caught a wave
with ben kingsley
both of us
rushing together
in identical liquid flow
joined by a deep
connection
to things vishnu & cosmic
surrounded by powers in towers
of luxury rooms
built by modern serfs
& paid for by colossal coffers
of continuous
casino cash flow
stimulated by
simulated lapses
of synapses
& dualistic winner loser
illusions
now one world
one mind one heart
one wave
all rushing all arriving
all floating all smiling
in the same
universal
space

take this pill

may it serve you well may it cure your ills
& make your alpha-delta-omega blues go away
may it give you great placebo & high flying dreams
may it elevate your test scores
raise your iron levels & get your gravy train
back on the tracks may it clear your spots
whiten your smile reduce your behind
& better define your abs & future
may it improve your sex life
expand your leisure time stop the world
& give you the power to manipulate
the quantum universe

take this pill may it serve you well
may it send you a better all-terrain vehicle
more comfortable shoes & a good book
may it pay your rent & speeding tickets
your credit card & your union dues
may it make you cooler than the other guy
the envy of your circle may it make you
young & rich & beautiful give you
super-hero strength & comic book x-ray vision
may it offer you hassle-free immortality
& no-strings-attached love

take this pill may it serve you well
may it make you famous & popular & help you
see the absurdity of being famous & popular
may it improve your sense of timing & humor
give you outer efficiency & inner peace
may it help you save the world from itself
may it be the one pill that turns your life around
so you can stop your cockroach scurrying
your mad reflex knee-jerking
& begin to become the luminous being
you've always already been

before you started
to take this pill
may it serve you well

perfect dervish girl

she spins & swirls
for a living around & around
she keeps on moving
does she ever touch the ground?
a whiz a blur a whirl a blink
she moves & shakes &
gives & takes
& makes & molds & spins
amber waves into silver & gold
around & around she goes
if she stops nobody knows
she isn't bothered
with time or tether she turns
him on then turns him
down then inside out she's on the town
but never about she drives
she flies does she ever unwind
(some say she even spins
from within) around & around
she wheels & deals & whirls & wins
she builds & gilds
& raises the bar
she's a wonder a woman
a stunner a blink
a wave a blur a curl
she's the perfect
spiral dervish
girl

this cordless pull

of belly-button gut wrench
this endless connection to corkscrew birth
this happy weightless wait
that lifts us into
& through
clockless time & space   .

these lines entwined that sail the seas
of deep relationship
that keep the secrets of our optimystic DNA
& grow the fins we use
for submarine wingless flying

this pattern of everything & nothing
& nothing & everything
of holding on & letting go
& arriving wildly strongly kindly
for each other

these prehistoric doors of perception
we open & keep open
those windows
that bring us ancient ocean air
& soft new moonlight
this holy portal for swimming
in the blood of each other

this wantless want on the river
of wisdom that moves us
to the borderless bankless place
without dualism
or death
into the open arms of galaxy swirl
this sweet embrace this kiss
this taste of forever
                    & you

unorthodoxical

he practiced sitting lying down
& it never occurred to him
he was doing anything
                              wrong
not thinking he thought
was difficult enough
without the physical strain
of position or posture

sometimes in deep meditation
he fell asleep
& after a good snore abruptly said
                a power nap
        never hurt nobody

not much of a follower
he enjoyed following his breath
in & out of the cosmic flow
a circular energy
developed momentum
& might
            until kundalini exploded
out of his chest
through the roof of his head
& radiated everywhere
as he flew around the room
his body limp on the bed
unconcerned with knees or back
or the petty opinions
of others
                perhaps he'd fly across
        the border to see her
perhaps today he'd even
leave the building

healing advice

ignite delightful incense
sandalwood will do
boil clean water
add fresh lemon & fresh ginger
steep 15 minutes
pour
          sip slowly from mug
warm hands
blow on restorative liquid
follow life of rising
steam
                watch clouds
          watch time
breathe deeply
stir in honey or sweet memories
meditate on illusion
watch thoughts come
& go
                hug your children
          lift spirits
laugh at seriousness
open heart open window or door
include unpolluted air
new awareness
          & play

the shaman speaks

the one who comes to you slowly will last
the one who comes slowly will last
the one who flows into your life
will pour through you
pour through you
slowly slowly soar through you

but marry yourself first
fuse heaven & earth in yourself first
fall in love with yourself first
life is eternal & death a dream
life is eternal & death a dream

choose the one who comes to you slowly
you will know when you stop thinking
you will know when you stop thinking
open wide open deep open deeper
& you will know the one
who comes slowly

life & death are the same dream
life & death are the same dream
both here & now both hear & now
yet one is always on the other side
one always on the other side

one is always greater than two
one is always everything
one is always everything
you can divide a pie an ego a nation
but you can't do math on god
you can't do math on god

remember your alphabet is backwards
remember we're reading upsidedown
close your eyes & open wide

dive deep into the dream
close your eyes & open wide
dive deep into the dream
dive deep into the dream

cartoon

a blank thought bubble
followed the master

everywhere

empty mind happy heart
he reminded us

sometimes two
        or three staggered
                        bubbles
hung over his head
fixed to the page

as if he could step on each one

        & walk out
of the frame

60 years to realize

the race is not about time
speed distance or even winning
although winning has its pleasures
however fleeting
        the race is not a race at all

the race is a ceremony a rite a ritual
a cultural event like a dance a play an illusion
for amusement
        a facade for essential symbols:
preparation comradery & friendship

showing up
        simply being there
                in that sudden moment
when gun fires
time stops
the rest of the universe recedes
then disappears
while you & your friends play
in another dimension
far from the madness of worldly survival

the race is also about escape
departure diversion creation recreation
& eventually arrival

            intuitively one knows
every step glide stroke or stride
        every turn obstacle bump & breath
a celebration
not about place prestige
or the polarity of winning & losing
but a legendary display
of personal spirit
        & wholehearted
      collective euphoria

the man who thought he was in control

cast his bread upon water
his fly into the river
made his world waltz
against the current
jig in the sunlight
froog in the shallows
can-can like no one else can

until a nibble a strike a bite
the flight & hook
lodged in his jawbone
found shelter in his ribcage
felt at home in every bone
he swam against
the flood of emotion
leapt out of liquid into sky
tried to fly away but fell
changed direction
sudden stop
          wriggled & thrashed
in frantic dance
to spit out the barb the line
the web the text the message
the email the stroke the kiss the splash
the wish
went slack then taut
& jerked as if she flipped reality
to reel him in
while he gasped for gods
to save his cold-blooded soul

control the furthest word
from his mind
right now he needed to be swept up
in her net
with kind words & private touch
murmuring the mantra of ages
catch & release
  catch & release
    catch

        & release

in my dream

                    i fall
          in love
with someone who wants
to hold my hand
                    when i wake up
she's still there
even her hand in mine
still there

          but then i realize
i've been living alone for years
so i know i'm still
dreaming
                    some days i don't want
                    to wake up
          some days i spend
most of my life
                    dreaming
          a steady stream
of dreams
for the one inside who holds
my hand
          dreaming her
          into my life

powers

i'm regaining my powers he said
improving my energy
& getting into
my flow

i can tell you've grown lately she said
you've had a chance
to live alone

it's different not having to carry
someone else's baggage he said

everyone has it she said
but we all need to carry
our own

either carry it or let it go he said
now i'm off to the gym
to let go
of some baggage

we must keep up
appearances she said

he said i look much better
than i appear

in their dreams

in his dream he is taller & richer
smarter thinner funnier happier
famous but not too famous
drives a green sports car
flies first class & never waits in line
someone else fills out his forms
he sees through walls
& predicts the future
doesn't crave power sex or money
holds everything in balance
because he lives by the sea
overlooking mountains
& beach with surf & warm water
with someone kind compassionate
spiritual beautiful funny
healthy wonderful honest
open & soothing
in his dream

in her dream she is younger
prettier happier wiser less emotional & thinner
she doesn't crave chocolate or ice cream
or attention
her legs longer
her skin tan & taut
foresight 20/20 & her children grown
& successful
her home not lonely
she walks every morning to the beach
for a swim
& the whole world is kinder
she's found her purpose
she's at peace with her parents
accepts her own death
because her husband still loves her
like the first time they kissed
in her dream

three women

you're a love poet she said
& i fell in love with her
but she wasn't ready for love
                    so i wrote a book
about desire

she said teach me everything you know
i told her i don't know much
& i fell in love with her
but she didn't notice
                enough
                so i wrote a book
about death

give me your number & i'll write you a song
i said to a senorita in a mexican cantina
so we fell in love got married
& later divorced
                    this time i didn't write
                    a book

        might never finish
that song

repeat relapse retreat

suffering impermanence & non-attachment
suffering suffering letting go
letting go
  nothing lasts forever
  suffering itching wanting
scratching grieving leaving
nothing is easy easy easy
empty empty empty suffering suffering
inside a magic bullet train named
desire whoooooossssssssh
this too shall pass
even impermanence will pass
even the letting go will pass
     everything in flux
   everything in flow
  everything but the suffering
& her perfect kisses
the permanence of impermanence
the permanence of impermanence
bridges fixes pieces hasta la vistas
texas stitches on paris dresses
our selfish lists of christmas wishes
the endless pitches for excessive riches
all the misguided glitches of triple sixes
mixed into the dead certainty
of change
everything except
   her delicious kisses
always on the tip of the taste of my lips
& the touch of her tongue
discovering my unnumbered suffering
my wondering stuttering puckering suffering
my godforsaken guzzling & blundering
my holy & profane offering

    our endless forever letting go
    of desire
forever letting go of my non-attachment
to suffering
suffering suffering
how everything comes & goes
with this blissful wishful
symbol suffering

the heart of healing

treat yourself to a retreat
away from the braces & battles
of shackles & hassle

let go of the loons & balloons
step away from boardroom typhoons
delete anxious afternoons
abandon the jungles of buffoons
& tune out the baboons
of cartoon saloons

retune regroup recoup
get back to the heart the core the root
back to the beginning of basis
return to the internal
to the cradle of eternal
the source of original oasis
heal yourself with homeostasis
heal yourself with homeostasis

do what nature does
when she needs a revolution
slow down
refuse reduce undo
slow down completely
away from needy greedy speedy
crazy busy dizzy

slow down completely to easy
to easy & dreamy & hazy
& let perfect grace embrace us
heal yourself with homeostasis

heal yourself with homeostasis

what cannot be said

will not be found in print
but scrawled on walls
& painted over
next week
as if nothing ever happened

what cannot be said
is a dreamstate
more real & disturbing than you
can imagine
there are always three doors to open
only i never have time because
the second is locked
& i spend all efforts trying to break in
which wakes me up
thinking about
what might have been

what cannot be said
has all been said before
but much better
by an unknown poet
in a cave near the border
i drove by him on my way out of tibet
they don't translate him
into your language
but you can read the manga version
which is more about pictures
than words

what cannot be said
is sold on TV
too early in the morning
after the airwaves wave goodnight
they'll double your order for free
if you pay shipping & handling

but wait
there's more

          what cannot be said
is discovered in music
those ever-elastic sounds in your mind
you don't understand
but intuitively
a great musician from another age
interprets your every vibration
exactly as if
          he's inside your head

unsettling
yet also wondrous
& you begin to wonder
if you
might be that famous musician
but for the sake of sanity
you must appreciate
the compositions
as if you had nothing to do
with them
          as if they flew through you
from the beginning
of time

sometimes i just write notes

to myself
so i don't forget the important stuff
      sometimes i write poems
to remember
tap into places long
forgotten
once dormant
& waiting for the magic world
where everything
makes sense
everything comes alive
where love conquers fear
& transcends earthly
atoms
      sometimes i simply want
to be me
silly little human goose
who knows less than
nothing
      sometimes when i remember
i am nothing
a blank slate in a universe
full of wonder
i can decide who i want to be
or if i want to be
anyone
at all
      sometimes no one
is the best one
to be

critical interlude

too clever too cute too honest
too beautiful too delicate
too tempting
too easy too sexy too spicy too lacy
too young too shiny too fancy
too racy too funny too happy
too bright too sunny
too sunday
too religious too dark too dangerous
too robotic too symbiotic too wild
too erotic too expensive
too free
too cheap too tight too curvy
too swervy too straight
too soon
too much too little too late
too thin too rich
too submissive too possessive
too aggressive
too prolific too vanilla
too dark chocolate
too pessimistic too realistic
too genius too delicious
too new too perfect
too perfect two perfect
too beautiful
too forbidden
too taboo
too me
too you

these poems these totems these omens

these quiet fragment puzzle pieces
unsolvable insoluble insufferable orphans
of every lost & tattered alphabet

interior tattlers telling on their author
offering broken pane wisdom

shards of holy fracture

reflecting smaller & larger parts
of the unseen
the unread the unnamable
great glass space of discovery
vanishing into the edgeless haze
of stirred or shaken
mixed drink metaphors

a good thing we write
to save ourselves

a better thing we write to make
& mend mirrors
not break
        or paint windows

chained to the stake

made of diamond steel
drove straight through the heart
of the earth
could only move four feet
in any direction
before collar offered
whiplash
            the sign posted close by
sent chills
down every mortal spine

yet one man
approached the beast
as if he knew something
no one else did
                hands out head down
        fearless
submission
slowly he walked up to the danger
of the creature

armed only with soft words
in low musical tone
            something in the animal
clicked

an old memory full of awe & trust

when parents were gods
& could do no wrong

she makes me want to play

electric guitar to the stars
she makes me long for lost years
realize a lifetime of love
in an instant of bliss
makes me blurst schoolboy words
of heart expansion
then makes me calm & zany
& fragile
      eternal
           she takes me with her
to talk to the dead
makes me forgive myself
& forget my mistakes
she makes me look in the mirror
& love myself
        she makes me
greater than my aging parts
makes me sing & dance
& find myself in downbeats
of heartbeat
    she plays with me
in the space
    between
      laughter

teaches me how to   arrive
in the moment
with &   without
   time

in the end the curtain falls

in the end the hero dies in his mother's arms
& gets reborn every spring
in the end
the end goes on forever
in the end a new story must be told in
the end there are tears
there's a big party with little sandwiches
& soft fragments of small talk
in the end you find out you know too much
of the wrong stuff
in the end destruction & cleansing
day turns to night
they kiss & make up
but nothing really changes

in the end heaven isn't anything
like you imagined it
cartoons are more real than you thought
you die because that's the nature of things
but you simply become
another thing
fading into the vast void
& nothing can be done about it
in the end you must say
goodbye to the ones you love
even the ones
who don't love you back

in the end forgiveness
becomes the only way out
in the end the way out
is the way in
in the end your life is important
it does make a difference
but it wasn't as serious
as you probably thought in the end

it's good to make them laugh
in the end you know
the beginning
is near in the end everyone
is anxious to go home

in the end your patience
will be tried
the color of your drapes won't matter
the type of car you drive will not be judged
your blood pressure pills
won't be necessary
& you realize life is what you make it
in the end you think
perhaps
clichés have their purpose
in the end the clock always winds
further down
yet you finally learn how to perform
with effortless effort
you feel life flow in & out of you
& everything else

in the end the hero rides off
into the sunset
the heroine gets her man
really another woman buried
deep inside her animus in the end
you see your life flash before your eyes
in the end you move
into the light
your friends & family
wait for you on the other side
in the end
you can learn a lot about illusion
& life from a mirror

in the end each regret becomes a dream
you learn if people really love you
in the end you cannot run away
& meditation is better than medication
in the end of the end you know less
than you think & more
than you realize
in the end thinking doesn't matter
in the end matter doesn't matter
in the end
the fat lady sings
if you can call that singing

in the end they usually give you
a few false endings
until you've had enough already
in the end they scroll the endless credits
of all the people you ever knew
& show all your bloopers
as if that's what they want you to remember
in the end
you leave the building & in the end
the lights come up
in the end

philosophy

i have said what i have to say & still

the words flow like a broken gas station toilet
& no amount of jiggling the handle
will ever stop me

i have said what i have to say & i know
it's not much but perhaps it's better than nothing
so many people & so many words
say nothing
or they swallow their important words
hide them deep inside
what good or bad does that do
where do they go when they want
to come out?

i have said what i have to say & although
i'm satisfied with my imperfection
i must not stop before my time
whenever that is
                  time & words go on & on
& on to somewhere where go
meets one
& nothing ever gone

i have said what i have to say & now
the rest of it is nonsense but i prefer nonsense
because it often leads us
back to our senses

i have said what i have to say & i'd sooner
not say anymore except i must respond
to pretending to know something
best to acknowledge there's too much to know
to really know anything at all

i have said what i have to say & yet
it's far far too late to stop now

i have said what i have to say
a far cry from being finished or washed up
or dried up or dressed down or clowned out
the clown in me wants to make you laugh
but what's to laugh about?
the world gets darker & darker everyday
perhaps it's time for a bright yellow
black comedy

i have said what i have to say he said
to punctuate & reiterate the parry of his thoughts
but who am i trying to fool
everything is funny
if you see the big picture
pull away
from the close-up
& get a god's eye view of the universe

i have said what i have to say so blah
blah blah blah blah blah blah
blah blah blah is it bad enough yet?
blah blah blah blah blah
blah blah blah it could always get worse
blah blah blah blah blah blah blah
blah blah etcetera etcetera

i have said what i have to say so i'll kick back
& watch the wonder of the wheels roll by
these planets in perfect ellipse
& the slow-motion beauty
of galactic spirals in harmony
with the whole of the holy
& even immerse myself
in the harmonic change of violence

i have said what i have to say for now
but there's always another now
see here it comes hear it
hear it wait for it
hear it
comes again & again

i have said what i have to say & i wonder
will it fill you up with disinterest
or wonder
when you discover what i've said
what have i said
when i say i've said what i have to say

the surprise of no surprise

she waits for the call
that never comes

the edge of her imagination blossoms
into orchids of anticipation
knowing full well
as soon as her phone rings
this thrill will vanish

> the fact that nothing happens
> makes everything possible

soon a carriage from another century
will stop at her door
a dapper footman
announces
your presence is requested
> fill in the blank
somewhere you've always wanted
to go

each bejeweled fragment
a figment of fantastic
just waiting
> for your participation

when the phone never rings

death is that beautiful woman
(you don't think you'll ever meet & even if you did she wouldn't ever want you)

out of the blue
you find out death really truly deeply
loves you
& you can't say no
to the chance of a lifetime
so one night
she takes you by the hand
leads you
underground
to the basement of your dreams
that place when you were fifteen
where your heart skips
a beat
then three or four more
until it stops
altogether
& she gives you
that wicked mystic kiss
you'll never forget
where the whole ball of neurons unwinds
& you look at your life
the complete movie of emotion
in a flash
you tally your regrets
but she isn't one of them
no no no not her
she's everything you ever
needed

she's the beginning
& the end

he's killing all the buddhas tonight

one by bloody one
chopping off their ugly empty
peaceful beautiful top-knot heads

not worrying not
thinking not caring just saying
fuck you to the masters

then surrendering
to the rudderless way

dozens of lovers & lamas to lop off
hundreds of collected gurus
to lose
chop chop
five thousand blessed buddhas
dead on the roadside

slaughtered scattered & collected
haphazard in the gutter
of the shoulder

will he make enough time
to kill

his attachments

nostalgia is never enough

remember the good old days
we didn't need rose-colored glasses
hell we didn't even need glasses
we had interest in savings accounts
& bomb shelters to save us
from ourselves
& we still played games in school
like duck & cover
duck & cover

remember the good old days
we wanted leaders to be our daddies
we believed all the news was true
we knew we'd all have our own airplanes
& the sky had no limit
& the GDP had no limit
& nature had no limit
everyone could afford a ticket
to root for the home team
before we woke up
from the american dream
that good old capitalistic
bait & switch
scheme

remember the good old days
when we took our cues from music
fashion art dance food love
everything revolved around the song
walls tumbled empires crumbled
disputes mended wars ended
our gods played guitars
blah blah wah wah!
until drugs blended into blood
& lives destroyed for a high
too many lives destroyed
for a temporary high

remember the good old days
before waters got muddy
& chariots fell from the sky
before pipe bombs burst
& mister clean made us paranoid
& androids dreamed of electric
sigmund freuds before soap operas
& rock operas & mock sinatras
advertised surprise & holy genocide
& the next new bob dylan
that never arrived

remember the good old days
before the joneses
moved into the neighborhood
& there was nothing to keep up with
before the first crash
before the first upright dash
before the first heartbreak
before the first wedding cake
after the first honeymoon headache
before time & meditation mind
before innocence left the building
& green genes turned blue
before thorn & scorn & spurn
before porn & unicorn & the battle
of little big horn
before sitting bull & raging bull
& the pointless point of no return
before we were born
before we were born

remember the good old days
without debt or threat or reject
remember the good old days
when our cement was still wet

before regret or forget
remember the good old days
like they haven't happened yet
the good old days of the good old days
before the stories & tales of old
could even be retold
remember the pleasure & splendor
remember the endless perfect weather
the cool & temperate climes
remember all the better
ugly sweater woody woodpecker
buried treasure love-letter
tender times

the further back we go
the more we think we know
life's a long-winded twisted imprinted
liquid vivid anxiety tilted
variety show
a flowing row of narrow nows
the width of a trouser cuff
the depth of a cream puff
the length of a shoe scuff
the strength of a handcuff
& given enough time
everything dies a hero's death
wreathed in stealth & breath & myth
so nostalgia becomes
the new vahalla
but never is never ever enough
nostalgia is never
enough

he measured loss by

counting broken heartstrings
adding up & down
the current number of severed
connections & snapped
synapses

calculated how much
his large pumping instrument
designed to give & receive
was in disrepair

the tune of their relationship
still vibrated in his bones
yet the precise tuning
of this channel
now impossible to achieve

the heartsong
of their quantum entanglement
off key off color off
                    kilter

never the same
ever again

the man who cheated on himself

walked through life in a haze of compromise
made everything incrementally worse
by settling for just a little better
than average
rested narrow laurels
on the building blocks of fear

the man who cheated on himself
forgot to calculate how much more toxic
his marriage would get every year
show up in the baggage
he carried under his eyes
& the way his shoulders slumped
as his face turned to frown

the man who cheated on himself
pretended his love grew deeper over time
avoided scales & mirrors
& selfies
imagined his branches full of flowers & fruit
but only doubt & self-loathing
took root

the man who cheated on himself
decided he needed something unconditional
so he brought home a dog
then dreamt even the dog divorced him
& upon awakening he wondered
why his marriage felt
like an act of self-terrorism

the man who cheated on himself
believed his luck was shifting
instead of non-stop guilt he experienced
expansion & expiry
death by a thousand papercuts

life by amplification & submissive surge
even compared himself
to the gods

the man who cheated on himself
never saw it coming
underestimated the power of self-respect
tried to make a four-course meal
out of a pinpoint smidgeon
morsel fragment
crumb

& in the end only fell in love
with a lonelier version
of himself

what hole is this

that chills bleeds & burns & will not
be healed
won't allow closure
cannot know completeness
innocence or mindless
abandon
        always questions parameters
measures all sides
feeds on the past
estimates how much pain
one kiss will cost
                how much is that
wanton hug
holding hands might break
the emotional bank
in this empty hot or cold

he's a fireball meteor
she's an ancient glacier
& they refuse
to trust their hearts
                together they make
an ungodly hole
the longer they linger on that wounded spot
the more it oozes
the further away they freeze
& smolder
        the older we fail
the closer we rest
to ashes

gambling is for losers

suckers self-loathers
& compulsive nobodies
everyone down
on their luck
wants to win a little
wants to chase the dream
wants a taste
of the illusive lady
who delivers victory on a plate
sweet goddess of action
feeds the fire in our bellies
gives us the guts
to lay it all on the line
even though odds are stacked
the stack is leaning almost tipping
desperate for a tip or an inside
glimpse
because we don't know half
what we pretend
but we're suckers for the line
the form the flutter the green & gold sheet
the windfall the longshot
the trifecta of instant intuition
the poetry of promise
the mad potential
that one day something good
maybe even great
might happen

when i discovered

a new york times article titled
how to live without money

i said that's perfect for me
on so many levels
                two paragraphs later
it was brought to my attention

this lucid self-help essay
was in fact called

how to live without
irony

white noise looking grey

conversation sounding older heavier
tired overheard
     use only things
tricks only take you so far
eventually you have to shed skin
& look yellow or green
or sometimes dark almost purple black
in the mirror
    everyone says lighten up
life's a joke
as if the grim reaper has a sense of humor
maybe he does the way he keeps
hitting
my funny bone
    white noise looking grey
sounding down
sliding deeper into delta blues
even maggie's farm got no jobs
no more
all the plantations
moved overseas
    use only things he said
but poetic devices are vices too
not flesh & blood
not white noise looking grey
used to be red when i was younger
back when
    i could hear all the shades
of mixed frequency
& inhaled all the meaning
of random murmur

the wheel

i'm not on a wheel she said
i don't believe in linear time

i see what you mean he said
but my wheel has no spokes

a little worried today she said
i just looked into the future
& it was blank

that's a good thing he said
make it anything
you want

she said i wish the landscapers
would finish my potting shed

what's the hurry he said
you'll only get to another moment

order disorder blues

impressed repressed obsessed
over & over the curve the round the bend
the ride the hard edge cycle again
ignition drive ambition desire lust or bust
this roundabout recess excess success
grand human illusion of the saved
& damned the news the ruse the fuse
the muse & o these steep stark
deep dark indigo blues
melancholy me
melancholy you

under-confessed over-regressed
& impeccably depressed this sordid order
disorder far wandered & wide wondered
worldly wounded & mad squandered
freshly scrubbed & money grubbed
fumbled flubbed & ego-bluffed
this large aching broken hurt
this fathomless mashing heart alert
this siren song wails & cries
in mystic lullabyes
too much right is too much wrong
& o these steep stark
deep dark indigo blues
melancholy me
melancholy you

under-impressed by excess & suckcess
that chord this reward that holy recorder
that lord this lordy hoardy lady
amusing muse of yahoos & gurus
this worldly new world order disorder
our obsession with regression confession
& possession of the curve the bend

the sound & round of boundless love
& wonder over & over the ride
this life this soft haze re-order disorder
cycle round again & again
& o these steep stark
deep dark indigo blues
melancholy me
melancholy you

bark Bark! said the dogma

bark-bark bark bark Bark!
go away & come again some other day
when you're ready to play
by the rules i say

bark Bark! said the dogma
scratch my back & stroke my throat
rub my belly & tell me
how beautiful i'll always be

bark Bark! said the dogma
i'll guard your gate till kingdom come
fill your plate with blinding faith
& my will be done

bark Bark! said the dogma
relax & have a drink or two
no worry no hurry
i'll do your thinking for you

bark Bark! said the dogma
you can sell the fountain of youth
from timbuktu to duluth
but only i can monetize the truth

bark Bark! said the dogma
i'll bite the hand that feeds me
because everybody needs me
to tell them what to think

forget about the drama mama
no one knows better than me
bark Bark! said the dogma
bark-bark into infinity

the man who was swallowed by an angel

didn't believe he was special
didn't understand his potential
why he got powers beyond his normal
or why his world
suddenly became more colorful
& a lot sadder

all the things he was taught got twisted
knowledge became an albatross
philosophy an endless not
money insanity
property a bad divorce
now all he could see was blindness
& cruelty
      the glass almost empty
          even judgement day loomed
          as another reality
yet still he believed
in the everlasting power of beauty

if only he could rub his hands together
spark a fire to look into the future
see his lover mentor & captor
pure or fallen
      did she have wings
      or always crawling without limbs?

if only he could see outside himself
& understand his whole part
in the plan
      if only his angel was ticklish
& he could escape in a laugh
or well-timed sneeze

what if heaven was worse
& the other side existed only to show him
all the pleasures he'd miss

when the man who was swallowed
by an angel remembered everything happens
for a reason
       he understood perfection
is only illusion
then illusion became both beautiful
& fleeting

he recognized the human condition as a paradox
& paradise is only possible if we don't
scare it away by trying too hard
or holding on
too tight
       if we don't complicate matters
         by force or confusion
            or getting too far ahead
               of ourselves

the man who was swallowed by an angel
began a new life all over again
& this time
he let go of the big red balloon
relaxed into himself
& had no need for reason
or why

effects of penance on perspective

my son is granted 30 minutes
of fresh air a day
the space about 20 by 30
the walls 12 feet tall
& only a small area of the yard
receives sunshine

the last days of summer linger
as i sit on my porch
listening to wind rustle through
turning leaves
that rush nowhere

seems everything sings a song
about golden summer light
how it shines & glistens
inside the deep ruby essence
of the wine in my hand

i can't remember
a more wonderful instant

until the phone rings

my son informs me matter-of-factly
the sun in his yard won't return
for six months

suddenly i turn silently inward

a fine bordeaux loses its flavor
the sunlight on my porch
now void of luster

raise a glass to decay

here's to the silent
one-way thief who steals
our narrow shallow youth
makes us stronger
yet more fragile brittle
flimsy-frail
            who rots floorboards
& scorecards & warlords
mildews edge & flesh
rusts each bridge & joint & hinge
calls in the cavalry
of maggots
to feast on waste
            breaks down greatness
sameness sweetness
& status
erodes every zenith
atom by atom
from shore to shore
dissolves the light of day
then murders the dark peace
of night
            offers the bittersweet
patina of age & change
delivers the mortal gift of loss
to eternal present
bequeaths the uninvited bequest
that cannot be returned
restored refunded
nor refused

keep death on your left shoulder

get to know him better
laugh at his jokes
listen to his problems
     become acquainted
         with his techniques
have a few drinks together
but don't pass out

make peace with his minions
recognize their voices
remember death isn't your friend
just make him think
he's your friend
     don't eat his cooking
         don't take his advice
refuse his pills
stay away from his girlfriends
detach from his couch
& lures
watch your back
lastly
whatever you do
whatever happens
     keep death on your
         left shoulder

you'll want him
when you need him

everything & nothing

everything has no meaning
everything is chaos pathos playhouse
disorder confusion
too many notes at the same time
massive muddled data
         overload
         overload
         overload
dangerous levels of facts
no room for more memory
cacophonous dischord
billboard chessboard springboard
ripcord
ripcord
ripcord

nothing is the definition of meaning
nothing has depth & clarity
nothing knows wisdom
perfection harmony & balance

if you achieve nothingness
you are a master
you'll always
        have all the answers
              answers
              answers
& nothing to do
& nothing to do
& nothing to do

dear one

thank you for sending
me that dream
last night
the way you wrapped me inside you
as i held on for dear life

you tasted me as i tasted you
& we dripped drop
                    by drop
into each other's ocean
never letting go of the wave never
crashing on any shore

we rode
        one perfect never-ending
pulsing fusing buzzing melting vibration of body
& tribe
becoming spirit becoming electric
        becoming eccentric
                becoming atomic
                        becoming flesh
& flow
        in the sleepless ether

all this tower babble

about fear of death & petty
immortality
all this mad sprocket hollywood
projection about your big brass sunset
boulevard star on the ground
to punctuate
lower case history
        all this jockeying
for position & reputation
on horses that never finish
      all this fleeting yearning
for a timeless masterpiece
that always runs out of money
& fashion & time
when we only want a word or two
to soothe the inner beast
a word or two to help us move
through molecules of woe
             what we really want
is a mantra that captures release
gives us a color that cleans the wound
& sutures the world
puts your finger on the trigger
of pleasure
      recalls the old vibration
      that makes us whole
& sees the holiness
in everything
        everything high
& lowly everything cosy
above & below me
everything flowering flowing
& sacred

don't laugh at me

for believing in something
greater than myself don't laugh
at me for thinking of a day
of reckoning
   please don't laugh at me
for praying for an answer
don't laugh at me for dreaming
a bigger dream don't laugh
at me for warning you
of the future
please don't laugh at me for talking
to the angels don't laugh
at me for asking for forgiveness please don't
laugh at me for acting
extra humble
or being mostly thankful
please please don't laugh at me
for depending
on poetry
   to the oblivious
   i am weak
to the weak
i am
a god

born three weeks late with a full head of red hair moved
to cali colombia at age two months (photo above: older
brother michael, mother & me) early mentors: howdy
doody tom terrific & mighty mouse grew up dyslexic so
my mother taught me how to read sports heroes: jimmy
brown willie mays bill russell muhammad ali & gordie howe
learned to please my father by swimming fast studied
the gospel of vincent van gogh remember the overnight
canoe trip at camp chikopee studied fred & ginger father
bought a classic seeburg juke box older brother ran away
from home & left me bob dylan's greatest hits moved
to vancouver saw jimi hendrix the doors soft machine
& the mothers of invention discovered pop art dada &
marcel duchamp zeke pfiffittt gave me a book on yoga
& i learned to meditate met duke ellington andy warhol
jorge borges r. crumb pierre trudeau allen ginsberg & joe
dimaggio first divorce rode my ten-speed across canada
studied samuel beckett federico fellini arthur erickson d.t.
suzuki salvador dali dylan thomas thomas pynchon tom
thompson bill hicks bill bissett & walt whitman studied
autobiography of a yogi visited burma tibet cambodia

145

& india birth of first son birth of second son birth of spiritual demons death of george harrison bought a camera & contemplates sky trees water signs shadows reflections & impermanence second divorce father gets dementia father dies continuing education: left bank bordeaux goat cheese & eggplant dosas i heart new york new orleans new zealand new shoes new music new books new poems new memories old friends old trees old movies & old patterns

StephenRoxborough.com

additional poetry collections
by stephen roxborough

the DNA of NHL (2017)

ode to radio nola (2017)

a beginner's guide to vital trivia (2016)

even bob dylan sometimes
must have to stand naked (2016)

bob dylan's 853rd nightmare (2015)

drinking with the ghost of dylan thomas (2015)

open heart sutra surgery (2013)

luminosophy (2013)

this wonderful perpetual beautiful (2011)

son of blurst (2010)

blurst (2008)

impeach yourself! (2006)

so far all the very important
mind-expanding long ones (2002)

spiritual demons (2002) CD

making love in the war zone (2001)

acknowledgements

no earthschool would be complete without a partial roster of teachers & mentors:

Jeff Pew (for reading listening guiding & cutting thru the BS) **Jim Bertolino** (for inviting me into his salon where i first learned to thicken my skin & sharpen my poetic skills) **George Gordon Byron** (for capturing my attention in grade 12 english) **David Ossman** (for being such a great reader he made me a better listener) **Sam Hamill** (for teaching me kindness & humility in his own abrasive way & urging me to reflect on the lineage of my poetics) Grandfather **Augie Carlson** (who believed in the power of the word) **Karl Blau** (for his generosity to community) **John Oughton** (for culling some poems from my death collection so i could place them in earthschool) **Anthony Burgess** (for wordplay & superb compound-hyphenated words) **Alicia Winski** (for helping me believe in the orphans of this collection) **Dylan Thomas** (a marvelous musician) **Henry Penner** (who made me read shakespeare out loud to his grade 10 english class not as punishment but as a teaching tool) **Charles Bukowski** (for raw oceans of open candor) **My father** (for teaching me to strive for excellence & finish strong) **Samuel Beckett** (maestro of rhythm & timing through repetition & pause) **Larry Kappel** (extraordinary professor of whitman dickinson & poe) **Walt Whitman** (cosmic father of free verse & the beats) **bill bissett** (master of inclusion expansion & radiant love) **Milo Duffin** (for his talent patience collaboration & ginormous suitcase of fonts) **Dale Winslow** (fine writer sharp editor big heart generous spirit) **Zak & Eli** (my sons my blood my incomparable teachers)

NeoPoiesis: *a new way of making*

1) in ancient Greece, poiesis referred to the process of making: creation - production - organization - formation - causation

2) a process that can be physical and spiritual, biological and intellectual, artistic and technological, material and teleological, efficient and formal

3) a means of modifying the environment and a method of organizing the self, the making of art and music and poetry, the fashioning of memory and history and philosophy, the construction of perception and expression and reality

4) an independent publisher with a steadfast goal to print and promote outstanding poets, writers and artists who reflect the creative drive and spirit of the new electronic landscape

NeoPoiesisPress.com

CPSIA information can be obtained
at www.ICGtesting.com
Printed in the USA
FSOW02n0836240317
32196FS